I Can Work!

Sharon Coan, M.S.Ed.

I work.

I get a work **chart**.

My Work Chart

Devan

Jobs	My Stars				
feed dog					
make bed					
dishes					
clean room					

I feed Sam.

I get a star.

My Work Chart

Devan

Jobs	My Stars				
feed dog	⭐				
make bed					
dishes					
clean room					

I make my bed.

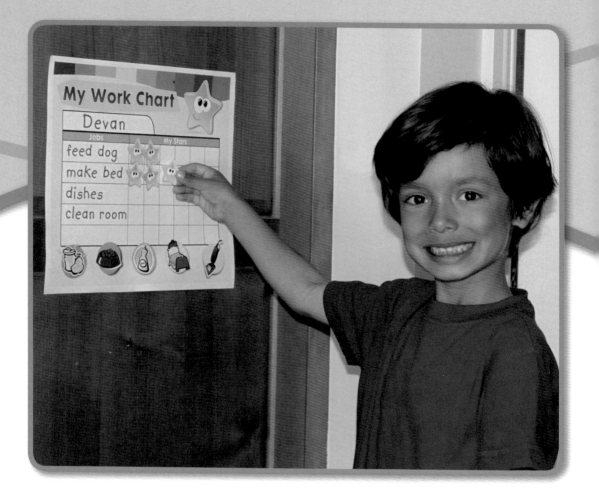

I get a star.

I help Mom.

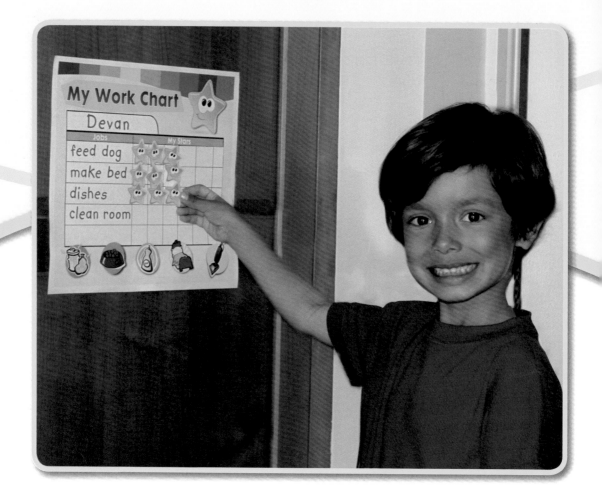

I get a star.

I feel **proud!**

Chart It!

1. Get your supplies.
2. Make a work chart.

3. Do some work.

4. Add stars.

Glossary

chart—a list

proud—to feel happy about something you have done well

work—to do a job

Index

Your Turn!

What work do you do at home? Draw a picture.

Consultants

Shelley Scudder
Gifted Teacher
Broward County Schools

Caryn Williams, M.S.Ed.
Madison County Schools
Huntsville, AL

Publishing Credits

Conni Medina, M.A.Ed., *Managing Editor*
Lee Aucoin, *Creative Director*
Torrey Maloof, *Editor*
Lexa Hoang, *Designer*
Stephanie Reid, *Photo Editor*
Rachelle Cracchiolo, M.S.Ed., *Publisher*

Image Credits: Lexa Hoang.

Teacher Created Materials
5301 Oceanus Drive
Huntington Beach, CA 92649-1030
http://www.tcmpub.com

ISBN 978-1-4333-7350-3
© 2014 Teacher Created Materials, Inc.